Living in SPACE

by Judy Nayer

Modern Curriculum Press
Parsippany, New Jersey

Velcro® is a registered trademark of Velcro Industries B.V.

This book is not intended to be an endorsement or criticism of products described herein.

Credits

Photos: All photos courtesy of NASA, except 44: ©1993 Paramount/Motion Picture & Television Photo Archive.

Cover and book design by Liz Kril

ISBN 0-7652-0890-3

Printed in the United States of America

6 7 8 9 10 11 12 13   07 06 05 04 03 02

Modern
Curriculum
Press

Pearson Learning Group

1-800-321-3106
www.pearsonlearning.com

CONTENTS

CHAPTER 1

The SPACE SHUTTLE

Have you ever wondered what it would be like to live in space? In many ways it is the same as living on Earth. People in space eat, sleep, and celebrate birthdays. But they also drink floating blobs of juice and never drop anything on their toes. There are only a few people living in space today. But in the future there could be thousands of people.

Astronauts ready to board the space shuttle

The space shuttle takes off from Kennedy Space Center in Cape Canaveral, Florida.

This book will answer many questions you might have about what life is like in space today. So climb aboard a space shuttle. Find out what it's like to move, eat, sleep, get dressed, work, and relax in the weightless world of space.

Where does the space shuttle go?

The space shuttle orbits about 200 miles above Earth. It takes only 90 minutes for the shuttle to go all the way around Earth. It can circle the earth 16 times a day!

The space shuttle in space above Earth

What does going up in space feel like?

When the shuttle takes off, the astronauts say it feels as if they are on a giant roller coaster. In orbit the shuttle flies very fast—five miles every second, or 18,000 miles an hour! Astronauts don't even feel as if they are moving. When the shuttle lands, it's a lot like landing in an airplane.

Space shuttle landing

Gravity GRABBER

The space shuttle goes from weighing 2,000 tons to 200 tons in 7 1/2 minutes! At 7 1/2 minutes after liftoff, the huge fuel tank is almost empty, making the shuttle much lighter.

CHAPTER 2
BEING WEIGHTLESS

Celebrating your birthday in space would be very different from what you might do on Earth. For instance, your birthday cake would be floating in front of you. The candles could not be lit because astronauts must be very careful not to start a fire aboard the shuttle. You could not cut the cake unless it was fastened down.

Your friends could still sing "Happy Birthday." Voices are almost the only things that are not changed by being weightless in space.

An astronaut practices being weightless in a special "zero-gravity" aircraft.

What does "weightlessness" mean?

Far out in space, everything is weightless. This means that people and objects have almost no weight. This is because there is very little gravity in space. Without gravity, there is nothing to pull people down and keep their feet on the ground.

What does it feel like to be weightless?

When people are weightless, they feel very light. They are so light that they float in the air! They can be upside down or right side up. It doesn't matter.

Does weightlessness make astronauts sick?

Some astronauts get dizzy and feel sick for the first few days in space. This feeling usually goes away. Some astronauts feel as if they have a cold all the time. That's because without gravity the fluids in their bodies move toward their heads.

stronaut Linda Godwin balances astronaut Jerry Ross
n one finger.

What happens to your hair in space?

Even your hair is weightless in space.
If your hair is long, it floats around your
head like a halo.

Do astronauts look different in space?

Astronauts look a little different in space. More blood flows to the face, so their faces look a little pudgy. For the same reason, their waists get smaller and their chests get bigger.

Do astronauts really grow in space?

Yes! Astronauts grow one to two inches in space. That's because gravity is not pressing on the spine. The spine relaxes and stretches. Back on Earth, astronauts shrink to their regular height.

What other body changes are there?

In space, bones and muscles get weaker. That's because muscles are not used as much. Even the heart becomes a little weaker.

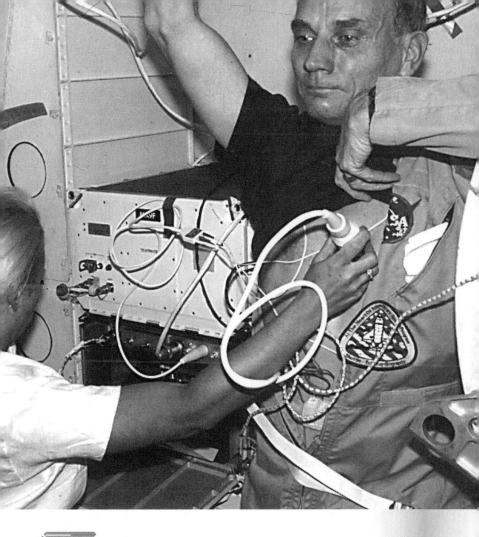

What can happen to the body after a long time in space?

Besides the muscles becoming weaker, the bones become weak, too. The bones lose minerals, such as calcium.

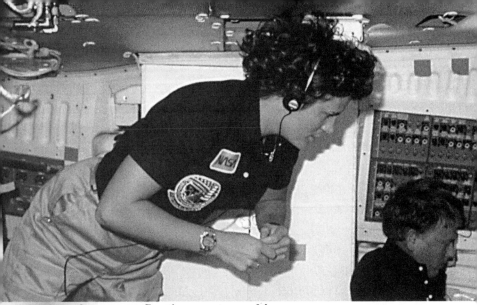

Astronaut floating across cabin

Can people move around in space?

When the astronauts are inside the space shuttle, they can float from place to place just by pushing off from a wall. They have to push very gently, though. If they push too hard, they might crash into a ceiling or a wall. If they bend over, they might do a somersault!

How are objects moved in space?

That's easy! Since nothing has weight, astronauts can lift heavy objects easily. They can even lift each other!

How do the astronauts stay still in space?

It is harder to stay still in space than to move around. The only way to stop moving is to hold onto something. The space shuttle has handholds and foot loops. The astronauts can also strap themselves to a chair or a wall.

How do astronauts keep things from floating around?

If an astronaut puts something down, it will just float away. All over the space shuttle, there are pieces of Velcro® to stick things to.

Gravity GRABBER

As the astronauts leave the shuttle after landing on Earth, a crew member stands at the door to catch items that the astronauts might drop.

3 EATING in SPACE

In space, astronauts miss their favorite foods. If astronauts get hungry for a banana split, they cannot go to the kitchen and make one. They cannot order out for a pizza! However, if they get a "snack attack" in the middle of the night, astronauts will not go hungry. It is just a little more complicated for people in space to eat than it is for people on Earth.

What do astronauts eat in space?

An astronaut's meal

Astronauts eat all different kinds of foods in space. Some meals are ready to eat and just need to be heated in an electronic oven.

Most of the food is dried, so it will not spoil. When water is added to dried foods, the food becomes sticky. Sticky foods stay on the spoon and will not float away.

How do astronauts cook in space?

The cartons of dried food go into a machine that spurts in water. The astronaut squeezes or shakes the cartons to mix them up. The cartons go in the oven if they need to be heated.

An astronaut adds water to food packets.

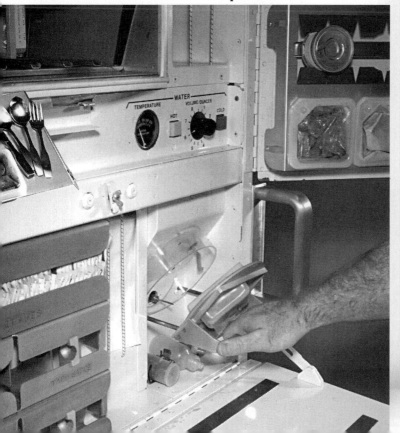

How do astronauts eat in space?

Astronauts strap meal trays to their legs. The trays have slots to hold the cartons of food in place. Their forks, knives, and spoons stay on the tray with magnets. The astronauts also use scissors to open the food packets. The astronauts eat together, but they don't sit at a table. Instead, they carry their tray tables with them as they float through their meal!

What do astronauts drink in space?

Astronauts can drink water, tea, coffee, and fruit drinks. But they can't drink from a cup because fluids won't pour in space. Astronauts drink by squeezing the fluid out of special bottles. All the drinks are powders until water is added to them.

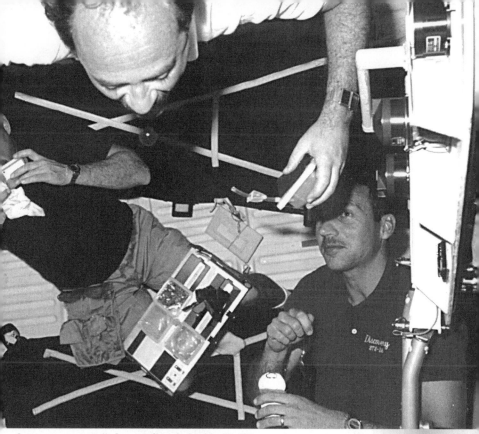

An astronaut "chases" a juice ball. The astronaut eating
has his tray strapped to his legs.

Do astronauts play with their food?

Yes! Astronauts love to play with their food.
One trick is to float a big blob of orange drink
and then suck it up with a straw. Another is to
float a cookie or a piece of candy and try to
catch it in their mouths.

Do astronauts have to wash dishes in space?

No! They throw away all the food containers, so there are no dirty dishes to wash. They clean their trays, forks, and spoons with a damp towel.

Astronaut Vance D. Brand stores trash after a meal.

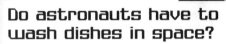

Gravity GRABBER

Did you know that tomatoes are considered a rare treat in space? Fresh fruits and vegetables are very hard to get. Astronauts on the Russian space station *Mir* had a feast when the supply ship brought fruits and vegetables.

4
KEEPING CLEAN

Everything the astronauts need to live and work with in space must be stored on the spaceship. Some things, like pencils or peanuts, are easy to store. Water, however, is not easy to store. Yet water is one of the most necessary things for people. How did scientists solve this problem? And how did they make the water stay in one place?

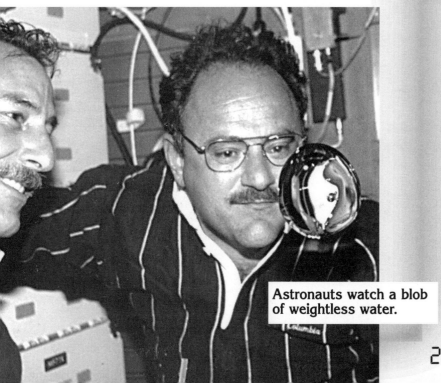

Astronauts watch a blob of weightless water.

How do astronauts wash in space?

In space, water won't pour from a faucet or run down a drain. To wash, the astronauts can take a sponge bath. They can also get into a shower bag. A hose attached to the bag sprays a mist of water. Astronauts use the mist to wash themselves.

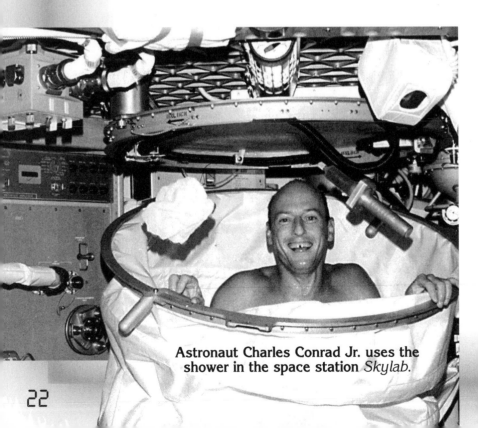

Astronaut Charles Conrad Jr. uses the shower in the space station *Skylab*.

Astronaut Robert Curbeam washes his hair.

How do they wash their hair in space?

Astronauts use a special shampoo that they don't have to rinse out. This helps save water.

How do they go to the bathroom in space?

Space toilets look something like the toilets in airplanes. However, the toilet has handholds, foot loops, and a seat belt to keep the astronaut seated. The toilet flushes with jets of air instead of water.

How do they brush their teeth in space?

The astronauts use regular toothbrushes like those used on Earth. When they brush their teeth, they have to be careful where they spit out water and toothpaste. They don't want it to float around the cabin.

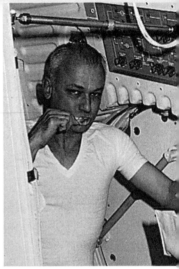

Astronaut Bruce Candless brushes his teeth.

Gravity GRABBER

Even though they are living and working in a small space, astronauts like their privacy, just like anybody else. If someone wants to change clothes, the other astronauts might stay in a part of the shuttle that is away from the main area.

CHAPTER 5

GETTING DRESSED

One of the first things little children learn is how to dress themselves. If a child grows up to be an astronaut, he or she has to learn how to dress all over again! Some clothing, such as shoes, cannot be worn, because it is easy to kick someone when everyone is floating around.

Clothing is hard to lose in space, though. If you misplace a sock, chances are you'll find it floating right in front of you!

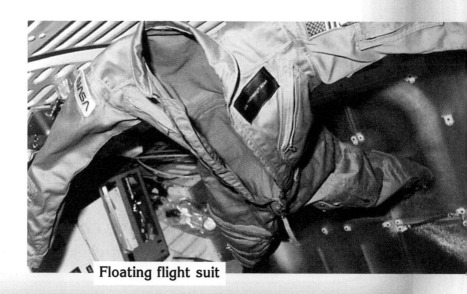

▲ Floating flight suit

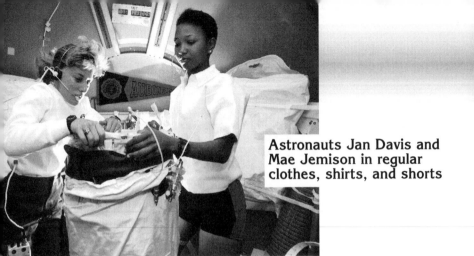

Astronauts Jan Davis and Mae Jemison in regular clothes, shirts, and shorts

What do astronauts wear in space?

Inside the space shuttle, astronauts wear regular clothes like pants or shorts and a shirt. The space shuttle has air that they can breathe, so they don't need to wear spacesuits.

When do astronauts wear spacesuits?

Astronauts must wear a spacesuit before leaving the pressurized module. First, an astronaut puts on special underwear, then a liquid-cooled undergarment, then the upper body part, the pants, the boots, the arms, the gloves, and the helmet. In all, the spacesuit has 12 layers. Maybe that is why putting it on takes about 45 minutes!

Do astronauts' clothes have pockets?

Yes! Astronauts have lots of pockets so that they can keep things from floating away. Astronauts keep pens, pencils, sunglasses, spoons, scissors, tape recorders, tools, small books, and snacks in their pockets. Luckily, none of these things weighs anything. Otherwise, their pockets would be very heavy!

Astronaut Bonnie Dunbar shows how she carries items.

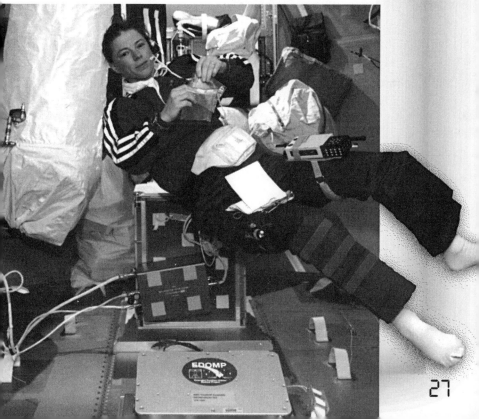

How do astronauts get dressed in space?

At first astronauts have a hard time getting dressed. It's tricky to put on socks while you are tumbling in the air. One thing astronauts can do is to put both legs into their pants at the same time while standing!

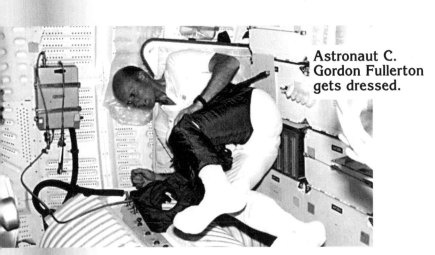

Astronaut C. Gordon Fullerton gets dressed.

Gravity GRABBER

Astronauts don't feel their clothing! Astronauts' clothes are really floating out around them, so they can't feel them. Astronauts feel dressed only when their clothes happen to touch their skin.

6

EXERCISING AND SLEEPING

A person must be very physically fit to be an astronaut. Astronauts train very hard before they go into space. It is important that their bodies be in good condition. They get plenty of exercise.

When astronauts go into space, they still need to exercise. How do astronauts exercise in space, where there is not much room and little gravity? They can't go for a jog or a swim or lift weights. After they are tired from exercising and want to go to bed, how do they keep from floating all over the shuttle?

Astronaut C. Michael Foale training on a treadmill

Why do astronauts need to exercise in space?

Muscles and bones that aren't used get very weak. Astronauts must exercise every day to keep their muscles, bones, hearts, and lungs healthy. To keep in shape, they need to exercise at least one hour a day.

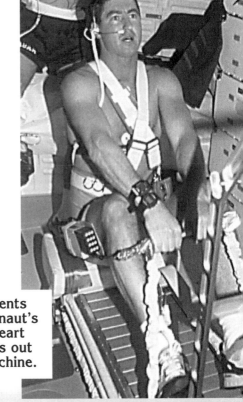

Special instruments check the astronaut's breathing and heart rate as he works out on a rowing machine.

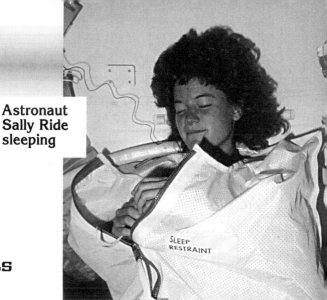

Astronaut Sally Ride sleeping

SLEEP RESTRAINT

How do astronauts sleep in space?

In space, astronauts cannot lie down in a bed. Astronauts sleep in sleeping bags that are clipped to a wall. The bag can be right side up, upside down, or sideways. An astronaut crawls into the bag and then zips it so that he or she doesn't float around. The astronaut is really floating inside the bag!

When do astronauts sleep in space?

Astronauts have a sleep time that is the same as on Earth. But in space, that doesn't mean it is night. In space, the sun rises every 90 minutes. Astronauts wear black sleep masks to keep the sun out of their eyes.

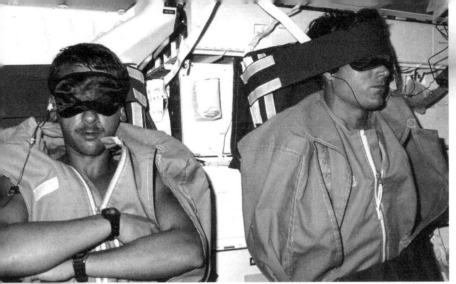
Astronauts Charles Walker and Michael Coats sleep on the shuttle.

Do all the astronauts sleep at the same time?

Usually everyone sleeps at the same time. No one has to stay awake to fly or watch over the space shuttle. Computers do all the work.

Gravity GRABBER

People in Mission Control on Earth are always watching even when the astronauts are sleeping. If anything goes wrong, they can set off an alarm that wakes up the astronauts.

CHAPTER 7

WORKING AND PLAYING

Jobs that are easy on Earth can be much harder in space. Have you ever tried to fix something, wearing five layers of gloves? Every day the astronauts have a long list of jobs to do. They conduct experiments, clean the spacecraft, and repair broken parts.

Astronaut Bonnie Dunbar checks an experiment on the space shuttle *Endeavor.*

What work do astronauts do in space?

Often, astronauts are sent into space to put satellites into orbit. They also fix satellites already in space. Different kinds of satellites do different jobs. For example, weather satellites take pictures of clouds and storms. Some satellites send television signals. Others help ships and planes find their way.

What experiments do astronauts do in space?

Astronauts do many kinds of experiments. They use telescopes to watch the stars and the earth. They use cameras to take pictures that help us learn about the earth.

Do astronauts make things in space?

Yes. Some metals can be melted together in space but not on Earth. These metals are used in making parts for airplanes and machines. Crystals grow much better in space. Crystals are used in cameras, telescopes, and computers.

Astronauts fixing a satellite in space

Do astronauts have to clean in space?

Yes! Every day they have to vacuum the filters that keep the air clean and polish the computers. Astronauts also have to dust with a special cloth. Dust, hair, and crumbs are everywhere. They must be cleaned up, or the air will get dirty and equipment could break.

Do astronauts have to take out the garbage in space?

If garbage were taken out in space, it would stay in orbit for years! All of the garbage is put into plastic bags. The trash is put in a special area and then taken back to Earth.

What do astronauts do in their free time?

In their free time, astronauts like to read, play cards, and listen to music. The astronauts' favorite thing to do is sightsee. Sightseeing in space means watching Earth. The scene is always changing, and the astronauts never get tired of it. It is better than TV!

What do astronauts see from space?

The astronauts have a beautiful view of Earth. They see blue oceans, orange deserts, and brown mountains. They see ice in the Antarctic Ocean and volcanoes in Hawaii. They see swirling clouds and flashes of lightning. They see a bright white sun, the moon, the stars, and the lights of big cities.

Earth viewed from the space shuttle

Can astronauts see the sun rise and set from space?

Each time they go around Earth, astronauts see one sunrise and one sunset. They can see 16 sunrises and 16 sunsets every 24 hours!

A sunrise as seen from the space shuttle

Gravity GRABBER

Long-distance calling by satellite was "invented" during one of the early space missions. Imagine a telephone call bouncing off a satellite before it rings a phone on Earth!

CHAPTER 8
GOING OUTSIDE

Astronauts like to go outside, but it is not as easy as opening the front door. They are going out to nothing—nothing but space! The temperature is different. There is no air and little gravity in space. If the astronauts are not careful, they could float away from the shuttle and start to orbit on their own.

An astronaut on a space walk

When do astronauts go outside in space?

Most of the time the astronauts stay inside the space shuttle. When a special job needs to be done outside the spacecraft, the astronauts go out.

What is a spacesuit?

A spacesuit is like a mini-spaceship. It protects an astronaut from the heat and the cold and provides oxygen to breathe. The spacesuit is thick and strong because it is made of many layers. The helmet and visor protect astronauts from the sun's harmful rays and from tiny particles speeding through space. The gloves have special tips that help the astronauts pick up things.

Astronaut in spacesuit

How do the astronauts make sure they don't float away in space?

The spacesuits have long, thin wires attached to them. Before the astronauts go out into space, they attach the wires to the space shuttle. This keeps them from drifting into space.

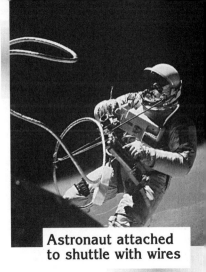

Astronaut attached to shuttle with wires

Astronaut Kathryn Sullivan wears a Snoopy cap.

Can the astronauts talk to each other when they are in space?

Yes. Under the helmet they put on a hat called a Snoopy cap. The cap has headphones and microphones.

Astronauts float through an airlock.

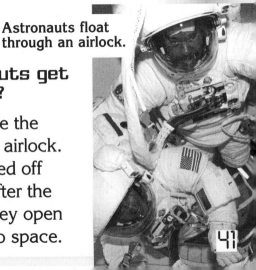

How do the astronauts get outside the shuttle?

There is a room inside the space shuttle called the airlock. The airlock can be sealed off from the main cabin. After the astronauts are ready, they open the airlock and float into space.

Astronauts F. Stony Musgrave and Jeffery Hoffman work on the Hubble Telescope.

How long can the astronauts stay outside in space?

The spacesuits have enough air and battery power to keep the astronauts alive for about seven hours. Usually the astronauts stay outside for two or three hours.

What kinds of jobs do the astronauts do outside in space?

Astronauts may change film in an outside camera or make repairs to the space shuttle. Sometimes they do big jobs like fixing a broken satellite. Other times they go outside to wash windows!

What is a jetpack?

A jetpack is a backpack worn by astronauts. It has 24 "thrusters" that give it power. It is to be used only in an emergency. If an astronaut has lost the wire that attaches to the spacecraft, the jetpack can be used to return to the ship.

Astronaut wearing a jetpack

Gravity GRABBER

Did you know that astronauts train for spacewalks underwater, wearing their spacesuits? The astronauts are really floating under the water, which gives them the same feeling they will have when they float in space.

CHAPTER

9

PLACES to LIVE in SPACE

Some day there might be a large wheel-shaped structure orbiting Earth. On this structure there would be schools, hospitals, factories, and apartments. Some people may live on this structure for their whole lives.

Before this day comes, many problems must be solved. Growing up and living in space is very different from spending two weeks on a space shuttle.

A future space city may look like this one from the television show "Deep Space Nine."

Space station
Skylab

What is a space station?

A space station is a spacecraft that orbits Earth and stays in space for many years. The space shuttle brings astronauts to the station and takes them back to Earth. The shuttle also brings food, water, air, and other supplies to the space station.

What was *Skylab?*

Skylab was the first space station launched by the United States. It stayed in space from 1973 to 1979. Three crews of astronauts spent time there. The longest mission was 84 days.

An artist's drawing of the International Space Station

What is the International Space Station?

The International Space Station is a giant space station that the United States, Russia, Canada, and 13 other countries are working together to build. It is called *Freedom*. Different parts of the space station are going to be taken to space and built there. When it is finished, astronauts will be able to live and work there for long periods at a time.

What was the *Mir*?

Mir was a space station that was launched in 1986 by the Soviet Union. Astronauts from many countries have stayed on *Mir*. In 1994 and 1995, astronauts returned to Earth after spending 438 days on *Mir*. That is the longest time anyone has lived in space.

In years to come there might be space colonies where millions of people could live their whole lives. Who knows? Maybe one day you might live in space!

Gravity GRABBER

Every two years, about 4,000 people apply for the United States' space program to be astronauts. Only 20 to 35 of those people are chosen to be in the program.

GLOSSARY

gravity (GRAV ih tee) the attraction, or pull, all objects in the universe have on all other objects; gravity holds people and things on Earth's surface

module (MAHJ ool) part of a spaceship that can operate on its own or as part of the larger ship

orbit (OR biht) the circular path an object makes around another object, such as the moon or a spacecraft around Earth

particles (PAHR tih kuls) tiny bits or pieces, such as dust

physically (PFIHZ ih kul ee) having to do with the body and how it works

pressurized (PRESH ur eyzd) made to keep air in a sealed environment such as a spacesuit

satellite (SAT ul eyt) an object made to be sent into orbit around the earth to perform a certain job, such as relaying communications

space shuttle (spays SHUT ul) a transport or craft that carries people, supplies, and equipment into space, usually to an orbiting object or station

structure (STRUK chur) something built or constructed, usually shelter or storage

weightless (wayt lus) having little or no weight